Where is My Right Shoe?

(You Say One Thing and I Hear Something Else!)

Billy & Cynthia Powell

CONTENTS

1. Intimacy
2. Romance
3. True love
4. Black love (men and women)
5. Dating
6. Toilet Paper
7. (His and Hers)
8. Divorce
9. Jezebel
10. Celibacy

11. House Chores

12. Loud Music

13. Mr. Fix It

14. Gas

15. Shopping

16. Listening

17. Why should I keep trying?

18. Grooming

19. Sex

20. Friendship

21. Loyalty

22. Emotions

23. Lifestyle

24. Insurance

25. Finance

26. Investing

MY INTRODUCTION!

Good evening, (imitating Alfred Hitchcock). Thank you once again for entering into another one of my 'Imperfect Masterpieces' zone. This time around I have been blessed and fortunate to do this project with the one and only and she's also my Author-Wife, Ms. Cynthia Powell.

So, let's get you up to speed regarding how we got to this point, and here we go.

A few years ago, me and Ex-Galfriend were scheduled to attend a wedding together, but we broke up before the event happened. So, one day I asked her did the couple ever tie the knot? And she informed me "Yes, they did and the wedding was really nice." Then she just out of the blue blurted out, "and going without you was like going without my right shoe!"

We laughed a bit, then I said, "Where the hell is my right shoe?" I played around with it for a while (because I saw a book somewhere in there) until I came up with 'Where is my right shoe?"

The second thing was, me and that same Ex-Galfriend had a conversation about toilet paper and the preferred way to hang it (that's one our topics inside & actually it's the catalyst that got the ball rolling).

The next thing was me and that Author-Wife of mine was having some off the wall conversation and she said something and I said something completely different but we came to the same conclusion. We just got there two different ways. And so, I said, "Hell, you said one thing I heard something else. But I still heard you, we just said it differently, that's all." Then she asked, "You said one thing but heard something else?" Whew, that took something out of the old brain cells (the few that still function).

And lastly, I knew that I wanted to write this from a male's point of view and I needed a female of the opposite sex to give her view and add some semblance of balance to my madness.

I called her and asked would she be interested in doing a project with me and I gave her a general idea of what I wanted to do. After hearing me out, she agreed to be the yen to my yang.

Now without further blah blah from me, I am happy to turn it over to my play by play partner, (oops, I was doing my White Sox TV analyst, Steve Stone impression). I am happy to turn this over to my ace and friend, Cynthia Powell, "Hey, Author-Wife, take it away!!!!"

Her Introduction

Hi, everyone when my friend who I affectionately call my Author Husband ask me to do this project. I told him sure why not. We agree to disagree sometimes anyway, so It was perfect! So, when we get together the shenanigans are never ending. We always manage to work it out in the end! I was very honored that he thought of me for this project. We for sure have different views on somethings and sometimes we even agree on some. Not many though! What a surprise! I hope you enjoy our different points of views. Maybe it might help you win some disagreements sometimes ladies! At

best help you work out a compromise!
Thank those of you who gave
suggestions for the topics.

WE DEDICATE THIS BOOK TO
EVERYONE OF

YOU WHO HAVE SUPPORTED
US ON OUR VARIOUS
JOURNIES! THANK YOU SO
MUCH!

*PEACE AND BLESSINGS! *

INTIMACY?!

It's so funny that we'd come right out the gate with this one. I thought that we'd work our way up to this kinda stuff. Oh well, here we go!

Personally, I believe that being intimate should be just that, intimate. It took me a very long time to even attempt to try to understand what it meant to be intimate as well as what would be required of me to fulfil the obligation of intimacy.

I didn't even look it up in the dictionary, I went out and asked a few guys of different colors, race and age what they thought about intimacy and its importance in a relationship.

They defined that intimacy to them was what ever their partner wanted. It didn't just have to be about sex. It really involved pleasing that special woman in their life. No matter what it was, they wanted to please them.

And not just to pacify her, but to learn about the things that she really like and take it from there. Yes, intimacy in sex is good, but the out-of-the bedroom (or back seat) is what really seems to count!

MACK DROP!

ROMANCE

Now, this one I didn't need to go out and take a survey for. I say that because I have been known to be romantic from time to time. Some women just bring it out of you. You'll find ways to take the simplest things and turn them into something romantic.

For example, take a rose for instance. We as males, usually give flowers to her when we done messed up or want to get out of the doghouse. But, what we can do with that same rose is on a non-descript day, pluck the petals off and put them in a bag and when you see her, start dropping the petals at her feet.

That's much more romantic than just putting them in her hands. And when she looks at you crazy, coolly tell her, "Doll, I'll get 'em up when we done."

Romance is really an essential part of the relationship experience. You don't really need some f'n counselor to help you figure some simple things out. Just take the time to attempt to be romantic and see where it lands.

I would so kick it with Alec Baldwin host of my favorite game show 'Match Game'!

TRUE LOVE

Again, no survey needed here. I remember not only my first true love but ever one of my true loves.

The first one was that puppy love thang. She was and always will be first everything. Even when we see each other after all these years, she is just as fine to me as she was then.

Then its that true love that you let get away. Hell, I'm still kicking myself in the ars for a handful of those misses. I had them but I was to much of a jerk to realize just what I had. But, when I run into them, I am oh so quickly reminded of just how much I gave away and allowed some other cat to be with my woman and raise a family with! True love ain't no joke, man. Especially when its over and the two of you know that it has run its course.

You'll still remember y'all's songs, movies, foods and whatever else, including that special smell that she permeated. In my cases of misses and losses, for the most part, we still remain friends throughout the years and decades.

TRUE STORY!

BLACK LOVE

What better love is there other than black love. I love being black and I love black women. Now don't get it twisted, I been in other pastures but I always wind up where I belong.

All three of my children, Brittany, William (BJ) and that Frances are by beautiful black woman who raised wonderful and dynamic members of society! We might not get a long at times or at all, but the reality of it is that they have proven their mettle.

Even for the other two who had a chance to have a baby with me, they went on and had children of their own and did great with them as well.

When dealing with black love, its not as complicated as it may seem. I'm quite sure that outside of our community they have the same problems. Ours is just in our face.

Here is my definition of true black love: Our parents showed us what black love was all about. At the time of printing, after over 50 years of marriage, my folks William and Gloria Bedford are still together living in the same house and sleeping in the same room and same bed (not the same exact bed from 50 years ago, you ninny)!

Viva the revolution!

DATING

Now, we all have been on the dating scene at one time or another, haven't we? We know that it's a rollercoaster ride of emotions. The ups and downs, the twists and turns, the highs and lows all play a part in the dating game (man, its been years since I been in that joint. Oops, I got side tracked again, where's that Author-Wife when you need her?).

Then you have the situation when you meet someone and you like them but they don't like you. Or they like you and you ain't feeling them.

Inside joke about me: I'm the king of the above, but, I gave myself the unofficial nickname of 'The Get It Right Guy', because I've met my fair share of women who have been through the worst of times before they get with me and they say, "This time I just got to get it right."

So, if you wanna get it right with anything like family, friends, yourself or God, give me a call and you'll soon be on the path to getting it right!

But, dating is still fun because you never know what's going to come out of the situation when you do happen to find the right person for you.

There's still hope for the Snaggled-Tooth Bandit yet!

TOILET PAPER

Finally, to the subject that was the driving force behind all of this madness. I am a strong proponent of the toilet paper hanging over the front. Because, I absolutely detest my fingers scrapping up against the crapper's wall.

That is so annoying to me. I don't want to have to fight with the wall and the toilet paper. My ex on the other hand prefers it against the wall. I thought that that was sheer madness. I really did, man. Now mind you, we weren't even living together or anything like that. But, we spent a considerable time at each other's place.

When we were talking about getting married and having to live together, the first topic was about having to have at least two bathrooms. We didn't concern ourselves with bedrooms, man caves and family space. "The bathroom is a man's castle, Peg" quipped the great Al Bundy! And I'm with that, too!

The greatest thing to come out of all of this was (naw, we didn't get married. Did you get an invitation to the wedding?), this nugget. (Look man, I choose to fight my battles and it ain't gonna be ova no toilet paper and how it hangs, ha."

Yeah, what she said, ha!

HIS & HER'S

Well, well, well, the myth of His & Her's (and yes, I did put an apostrophe on her because it's a fact that possession is 9/10ths of the law) dates way back to The Garden of Eden days. You see it was like this here, Adam was given dominion of the garden, then Eve was brought into the picture and with one bite of an apple, the whole concept of man having dominion over his house was blown in the wind.

Just like that it was over, man had to go out and fend for himself and his family. The running of the household fell to the woman while he was out getting that money to provide for them.

So, while he was out getting that bread(money), she was inside keeping it clean. Then one day she had an epiphany, and it went something like this, (thought bubble, like in the cartoons) "What is his is mine and what is mine is mine."

Once that law was passed down from generation to generation, it became quite evident that the proof was truly in the pudding. And, if said mister didn't conform to that law, he was subject to go without clean clothes, a clean house, a good home cooked meal and the occasional conference in the bedroom or back seat of the car.

That's my story and I'm sticking to it! Really, I am!

DIVORCE

Again, something that I needn't no help with. Coming from a family with both parents still very active in our lives, it wasn't in the cards for me to be married I guess.

Here's a lil ditty about Billy. I come in the door with a disclaimer, 'I ain't as good as my daddy, but I ain't as bad as your worse relationship, but I'm the best me that you can possibly get. I won't be needing your car to drop you off at work while I go home and chill at your house until it's time for me to pick you up from the bus stop. I don't need your money because I have some loose change laying around somewhere and it ain't in your purse or in your couch. And I don't need keys to your place because I already have keys to my own."

What I got was less than fifty-two weeks of same household marriage and about twenty-four months of it being on a piece of paper. When the love isn't there, its time to pick up and move on. No one was held hostage for years and decades just because they stood in front of family and friends telling one of the biggest lies of their lives. Hey, sometimes it works and other times it just doesn't. I happen to fall in the latter…….

Jim Cornette, the great manager of the Midnight Night Express said it best regarding one of his teams finishing maneuvers called 'The Divorce Court', "It separates your arm from your shoulder." Classic Cornette.

I'm a POW, a Prisoner of Wrestling. UWF, ECW, NWA & WCW!

JEZEBEL

Ah, good old Jezzie! She sure has made life difficult for a whole lot of families, mainly in relationships. No one is immune to her because she comes in many different forms, colors and smells. She appeals to our senses more so than our emotions. And once she's gotten that, it's a wrap.

She can be "The Clean-Up Woman" or "Jody Got Your Girl and Gone". She'll have you idolizing her and following her directives even against your better judgement, especially he if she doesn't get way. That's when she'll go for your very soul and existence.

Once you've crossed her, there is no coming back for forgiveness. She'll have you taken out at the drop of a hat or as quick as a snap of the fingers. We've been warned time and again about this one here, yet, we still insist on keeping her a around. Either, by friendship, marriage or child rearing and in some cases all of the above.

Its tight but its right!

CELIBASY

Okay, this one's probably gonna be a little short, but, I'm up for the task at hand (I'm still looking at the screen and all I hear is Us dog barking that interrupted the crickets in my head).

Think Billy, think.

To address this subject, you'll need to get a copy of "From Dopefiend to Deacon: Chasing a Pipe Dream". Then you'll see why I surely ain't no choirboy let alone an authority on the above subject.

One thing I ain't is a phony. In fact, the only thing fake about me is my teeth and I hate wearing them!

HOUSE CHORES

This is where the rubber meets the road. I have the experience of living with one female in my entire life, that in itself was an adjustment for me. I have always had a place of my own ever since I moved out for good in 1900 and 96, June of said year. I have been blessed to have more than enough space to live in including my studio apartment. That sucker was huge.

So, when I cohabitated, the ample space that I was use to became not so ample anymore. Empty closet space wasn't there anymore. The coming and going was regulated to a certain time.

I ain't never really been a domesticated cat, ever since OG Triple-Triple let me loose off of her apron, I been hopping over fences to see if the grass was truly greener on the other side ever since.

When it came to the house work we shared the work. The only thing that I refused to participate in was the shopping (of any kind, Christmas time is the only exception). I detest having to go in and out of aisle and stores with a passion.

That was hers and hers alone. My solo chores were the yard, grass, snow removal and car maintenance. The garage was off limits to her and the basement was off limits to me. In that sense we cohabitated very well. And there wasn't a problem with the bleeping toilet paper, either.

Gorgio Armani rules!

LOUD MUSIC

"Mama said knock you out. Destruction, terror and meyhem.." LL Cool J goes hard through my speakers. Followed by Tin City's 'Suspicious'. He sings, "Now your hairdo is a thing of the past.." How can you not rock out to this? Some joints are just made for being played loud. At home, in the car and for sho in the trusty old headphones. Mr. Fingers 'Mystery of Love' (dub version, 1900 and 85) is responsible for more than one set of high quality speakers rendered useless or reduced to giant twitters. Boom, boom, boom, boom, boom, boom, boom, boom……….

Then you have the Police singing "Voices inside my head" with that hard baseline and drum accelerator. I mean, come on man. Or the Temptations, 'Beauty is Only Skin Deep'. "She may be fine on the outside, but so untrue on the inside.." And what about Maroon 5's, One More Night, "Hey baby give me one more night. I know I said it a million times.." And hearing Christine McVeigh of Fleetwood Mac rocking, "You can take me to paradise. And then again, you can be cold as ice. I'm over my head. But it sure feels nice.."

But when you got a hard rider that likes the music loud and good, my friend, that one is a keepa! The two of y'all rollin and bouncing your heads to the funky beats. Or at the club looking crazy at each other when those certain joints explode through the speakers.

That's how we roll!

MR. FIX-IT

A couple topics ago, we talked about chores and I strategically omitted this one here because it in self deserves its very own section. I ain't that dude. I also come with another disclaimer, and here goes. "I ain't about that lefty loosie righty tightie life or that painting life, but, I'll see to it that it gets done." Everything else, I'm down with like cooking and cleaning.

I ain't never been good with troubleshooting and fixing stuff. I admire those cats that can get in there and get it done, I just ain't one of them. And I used to kick myself in the ars when I had to get the car fixed and stuff because I had an opportunity in high school to take up a trade like, woodshop, electronics, auto shop or drafting. But I was too busy trying to graduate at in other f'n ways.

Unfortunately, for dummies like me there isn't any future in that. It comes without a 401k plan, retirement benefits or health insurance. And people like me need all of the above and more.

It wasn't that I thought that any of them was beneath me, the truth of the matter is that I had Attention Deficit Disorder before it was even popular or a scientific/medical diagnosis. Just ask my parents and some of my former bosses and drug dealers.

Still scratching my head OVER THIS ONE, TOO!

GAS

They say that most relationships break up over, money, infidelity and loss of love. Well, they happened to leave one crucial element off the list and that being gas. Many a man and women done had that conversation about the car leaving the house full of gas and coming back on E.

I've seen it and witnessed it first hand and it wasn't funny at all. She thought that it was funny but even to this day I still don't get the joke. I told her, "If you 'bleep' runs out of gas, don't call me because I try to keep gas in the car. And you pass up a gazillion f'n gas stations coming and going." Needless to say, I never had to come and get her of the side of the road.

I don't mind riding over to Hammond and filling up the tanks because there is so much that can be done in between the two. And I ain't that bright, but I know that my car runs off gas and nothing else. When things change, then I'll revise this chapter.

I am so gonna get that! Ya dig?

SHOPPING

ANOTHER, touchy situation. The whole idea of shopping absolutely drives this cat crazy. I don't want to do it in person or online. The whole process is way beyond my pay grade. Take my father for instance. This man will go in thirty stores in thirty minutes! He'll leave out bright and early in the morning and be back home chilling by noon. Who does that? (eh, Amarie is killing it in those heels in her video, 1 Thing, but that thick chick in the silhouette and to her right is getting it crackin', wow. Thick chicks in heels, oh so rock!).

See, I need a diversion from the toil and doldrum of shopping. Take that baby sister of mine, Mel, the queen of online and walk up. Just like the old man, she'll have one of those shopping channels on for hours at a time. After ten seconds, I have officially checked out. Sometimes, it pays to have A.D.D and this is one of those cases.

Then they'll even talk about it. When does the insanity stop? And speaking of Sanity, they've finally made it up to the Smackdown Live tv roster (Erik Young aka EY is a certified head case and one of my favorite wrestlers of all time. And he is the only man to ever hold the TNA Knockouts(women) Tag Team title with ODB).

Let the Insanity begin!

LISTENING?

That sound that you are hearing is the wind blowing through my ears. Like the song, 'Dust in the Wind', by Kansas. Or Greg Allman's, "Midnight Rider" (my life's theme song), then I start hearing, "Brandy, you're a fine girl. What a good wife you'll be.." that's Looking Glass.

But, when Big and Rich starts rocking out to, 'Save a Horse, Ride a Cowboy' then it dawns on me that she is still yakking. Here it is, I done mentally checked out and she still at it. So, I start tapping into America's 'Horse with No Name' and then I start silently mouthing the words to 'Tin Man', "Well, Oz never gave nothing to the Tin Man, that he didn't already have.."

That's when the total act of treason is exacted, she grabs my only other lifeline, the remote control, and stands in front of the GD television.

And then she has the gall and audacity to asks me, me!, "Are you listening to anything that I'm saying to you?" and without warning, because I have been so rudely interrupted at the best part of the song, it comes out, "If I didn't have ears, I'd hear you through my nose.."

How can one argue with logic like that?

WHY KEEP TRYING?

I don't know the answer to this one here. So, I'll just ramble on and on about something or another just to save time, space and brain cell usage.

Personally, I'd rather be discussing sports, music, what's on tv or anything else (except for shopping and handyman duties). But, one can say that when you keep trying that someday all is going to be well and good. Then others can say that the more one tries the fewer results they get back.

I've been on both sides of the struggle a few times in my life. Love and relationships are a tough challenge for any one, old and young alike.

The last time, I kept trying, she wasn't, then when I stopped trying, she started. It was a little too late for both of us.

Then after we both had given up on trying, we still wanted the best for each other, but, it wasn't each other.

I didn't have to ask that MF to help fix my life. It was already BROKEN and all the king's men couldn't put us back together again.

Blah, blah, blah, blah, blah…………………….

GROOMING

Keeping it tight will never go out of style. No matter what port of life you are in. Take me for example, I started balding early in the game. But, MJ popularized the bald head look and I look many other brothers started rocking the bald eagle look.

The old man is in his 70's and has a head and face full of hair. The son is in his 20's and has facial hair that he routinely has cut off every week that we go the shop. I be like, I have to go a month without grooming to eek out enough facial hair to barely get a goatee going. And a beard, forget about it!

They say that sometimes a gene skips a generation, well, that must be true because the good looks gene, the stature gene and the hair gene from my old man all missed me and landed perfectly on my son.

In my defense, when I ain't looking like a bag man, I do clean pretty good. A couple of my bros, Denny and Darnell got killer clothes and shoe game and be watching 'em. But, Mr. Cleveland R Person, lay it down like no other pastor that I know. And yeah, I am being biased.

One day......

SEX

Some say that its overrated. Some say that they can take it or leave it. Some say that it shouldn't be done between friends because it will ruin a good friendship (I believe that, of course, if the sex is bad). But, I say sex is a part of life. You are going to do it one day and you may never do it again, but, you're gonna do it.

Sex is as much a part of or DNA as anything else. Not everybody believes that it is taboo. Not everybody believes that the earth is going to open up and swallow you into the abyss because you got down and dirty.

But as a heterosexual man, there is nothing finer than looking at a woman and thinking about what you want to do to her and that body of hers. Her walk, her touch, her scent and even her voice is what attracts us from the beginning. Oh yeah, baby, it gets real!

Sometimes we act out on it and sometimes not. I don't think that that defines who we are as a person. We are sexual by nature and we are the only living and breathing creation that doesn't have to have a season to be in heat and ripe for the picking.

I still have never sent an emoji in a text, ha!

FRIENDSHIP

A friendship is like an insurance policy. Some are long-term while others are short-term. I have some long-term friends from way back in the day. Like Monroe, Danny, Brian & Drew who I grew up with. Others from work like Leslie, Nate, Montez, Rodney and Darrell. Then the people like Cassandra, Tanya, Gloria & Tim Short, Dove, Dee, Diane & Mrs. Frances L Person who I met through the church.

While others that have played a just as important role in the latter years like Donna Lewis, Derrick Anderson, Derrick Warren, Larry Roberts, Sheila Carpenter, Frank Roberts, Omar Karim, Fareeda Watson, Joel Watson and Mrs. O. They all gave a brother a break and played a part outside of business.

And who can forget about that Jackie, Joyce Gye, Deborah Minor-Harvey & Tabatha Miles and Andre Ellis.

I said all of that to say that friendship isn't based on talking or seeing someone daily. But it's what comes out of it when you do get together.

Y'all just wore me out!

LOYALTY

Hey Cyndi, now that was a righteous way to segue into this topic about loyalty. You know what, that author-wife of mine, I tell you (notice the lower casing, ha).

When you are a friend you should be loyal to the friendship. There once was a really cool email about a couple of friends sitting in jail together laughing and joking about how much fun that they had getting caught. The jist of the matter is that loyalty lies deeper than the surface.

Did Nino Brown really just say? "Cancel that B, I'll buy another one." And I ain't even watching New Jack City...

Me and some people have sworn loyalty to the dirt and in one case, its been well over thirty years that the secret only lies between us two. Now, that's loyalty.

But, you have those who ain't loyal to nothing but themselves and that two is fine. Because it is a lonely place to be. I go to bat for those and only those that I KNOW will do the same. That's why my caper circle is so small.

She still in lower casing!

EMOTIONS

Is that referring to the song by the Bee Gees or that sexy black girl group The Emotions from back in the day? Oh, my bad, human emotions, eh?

Well, I'd prefer to yammer on about the groups above but I was steered in this direction instead. When dealing with emotions you either have thin skin or tough skin. I really can't say much about me having thin skin because I had to get thick skinned early in the game.

You see, I wasn't the most talented, athletic, attractive or smartest kid around so I was often either bullied, skipped over or just not excepted.

This stuff could've turned me into an emotional wreck or a serial killer. But, it helped me to be the best drug addict that I could possibly be.

Inside the haze and maze of alcohol, drugs and wonton sex, I was afforded the luxury of having my emotions numbed. Do get me wrong, I still could cry with the sinners and laugh with the saints. I still hurt over loss and revel in jubilee when the occasion presents itself. There is a time and place for everything.

Long live the Teddy Bear, Mr. Teddy Pendergrass (you may insert your music now)!

LIFESTYLES

Of the rich and famous? I ain't got that far yet (oh but my change is coming!). So therefore, I'll just press onward about the subject. There are so many different lifestyles to be a part of in everyday life. Career, status, family and business all play significant roles in shaping our lifestyles.

And the social groups that we interact with also contributes to our lifestyles as well. Like you can be a part of the Cognac Club, but I'm more of the wine off the vine culture, Richards Wild Irish Rose (Red preferably, White when a change of pace is needed).

The image and lifestyle that we portray is for what we want the world to see. Sometimes, it's carefully crafted and woven. Other times, it's a simple as the nose on your face. What you see is what you get.

Then the door closes and the blinds come down, that's when the real comes out. Some people say that image is everything and others say that it is the only thing...

Bobby Womack aka The Poet sang it best from his smash 'Nobody Wants You When You're Down and Out "Oh yeah, humm, Once I lived life of a millionaire, spending my money, honey, oh I didn't care. Takin' my friends out for a mighty good time, drinking that good gin, champagne and wine..."

And no selfies have I ever taken, either!

INSURANCE

I was thinking about this one but it was totally unrelated to this. Henry Ford and the assembly line car line rolled cars out like never before. Without even knowing it, he unwittingly opened up the country and culture.

After that, cars had to have identification, upkeep, gas, license plates and insurance. That last one blew up into a monstrous industry in itself.

Often times, we have insurance on our cars and little or none on ourselves or family. Isn't it funny that the law of the land says that you have to have insurance on the vehicle that you plan to operate? But there isn't any mandate that says that you have to insure yourself or your family.

OUCH!

FINANCE

"You don't work, you don't eat." Point blank. Soul Brother #1, Jams Brown sang to us about "Pay the cost to be the boss. Look at me, you know what you see?" That's from the movie Black Caesar's soundtrack.

A man should be financially stable. That doesn't mean that you have to be able to do everything that you want to do, but you can do everything that you need to do. It took me some time to get there but not only am I there, I plan on going further than that. My pops and my spiritual pops instilled that in me more than any movie star, athlete, rapper or wannabe gangsta could ever do.

This is showed by being proactive and not just reactive. Growing up, my sisters thought that we were rich. I on the other hand knew that that wasn't the case. I knew we weren't rich, but I knew that we weren't po' either. Baby, we had a charmed life, I can say that with certainty.

One Christmas eve, the tree was up but there weren't any presents underneath it. We went to bed without the usual glee and excitement of years past. I believe we cryed ourselves to sleep that night. Early the next morning we were awakened by our folks and led to the front room of doom. And we had the best Christmas, ever! Do you hear me?!

Hey Denny, did someone just say, American Express Black card!

INVESTING

This one I can attribute to my last job working for someone. When I became an employee, I had to get into some form of investment for my future. And living the life that I live, that's a tricky one in itself.

I sat down with the vendor and we began searching for the right fit for me and my money. I couldn't get stock in ECW or WCW, same for Richards Wild Irish Rose, Inc.

So, we settled for some low risk, long term investments. And after 11 ½ years of employment, I cashed in my chips and rolled out. I was amazed at what can be done if you don't touch it. It wasn't until they contacted me to see what I wanted to do with the money did the reality set in on me.

I told them to give me a day to think about because I had been paying off the IRS, Bankruptcy and Child Support for so f'n long that I wanted to take the money and run!

The agent understood my plight and assisted me in the right direction. Whew, and I was able to use that money to start my very own business.

Condoms used to cost $0.25 for 1 or 3 for $1, I didn't invest in either............

SPORTS

No music references needed here, at all! I could go on and on about sports because I love 'em! Hockey, Lacrosse, Golf, Tennis (only if the Thunder-Queen, Serena Williams is playing), Basketball, Football and the greatest of them all, Baseball (except for that bush-league team on the northside of Chicago and the pinstripes out east). Focus, Billy, focus.

When we get together, we boast about the Bears winning the Super Bowl, the Bulls winning 6 championships in 8 years, the Blackhawks' three championships and of course, the most important World Series win in history, the Chicago White Sox of 2005!

Hands down, the winner! Oh, I still got a half a page to fill out.

I couldn't imagine a world without sports, I probably would go off the deep end. I mean its only so much murder, mystery and mayhem that a brother can watch on tv. And sports, my friend is the tie that binds.

Not just neighborhoods but cities and states. Its nothing like calling a friend that loves a rival team and rubbing it in when your team squashes theirs!

Scott Norwood, I finally forgive you…….

CHIVALRY

Webster's dictionary definition reads as such, a gallant gentleman.

It doesn't take much to be gallant or a gentleman. Especially, if the chance or opportunity presents itself. What I mean is this, women have been opening their own doors and pulling out their own seats for so long, that when a guy attempts to do it, they are given a strange look.

Example, I picked up a young lady at her house and when we got to the car, I stepped in front of her and opened the door. She looked me up and down as if I was some sorta alien or something. "If you're with me, I'll open the door for you." She smiled and loosened up a bit.

Being a caveman works at times but sometimes listening to the Temptations,

'Treat Her Like a Lady' applies. "I'm the kinda guy who don't believe that chivalry is dead, no. 'Cus I believe a woman should be treated with the upmost respect. Don't be afraid. Don't turn and walk away, I wanna get to know ya.."

"Don't be afraid, don't turn and walk away. I wanna get to know ya. Don't be ashamed. Don't say that loves to blame. Just come and look me over. You'll find a heart that you have been looking for. How could anybody ask for much more. Now I like opening doors, picking up her hanky off the floor. Light her cigarette that she smokes, even help her with her coat....."

"Walk out or get carried out!" Otis Williams to David Ruffin.

FEAR

Fear ain't no joke, man. Its as real as real gets. I don't believe that any of us are exempt from it. The fear of failure, loss and even success are just a few.

But, when it comes to being a man, I think the pressure of that in itself presents itself. We have been given the charge of being leaders and go getters. We're suppose to be the pace setters and conquerors. The great providers and the one who can get it done.

This ain't a black thing or a white thing. It's a being a man thing. And when we fall short of those expectations, we fear the worse. We fear that people will think that we are weak or losers.

I don't think or believe that any father has tipped through the tulips without stubbing his toe and looking around to make sure no one sees him crying.

The fear of losing our identity should be on high alert. The fear of every thing else, is secondary.

No matter what this current society tries to jam down our throats, being A MAN will NEVER, EVER GO OUT OF STYLE!

DEATH

The big 'D'. The one thing that is inevitable for all of us. It's also the one thing that we all have in common. Ask Adolph Hitler, Pol Pot, Saddam Hussien, Kim Il-Sung, Jozef Stalin and Mao Ze Dong who individually killed 100's of 1000's of people, if death had a racial bias when their number came up.

Be it by one's own hand, at the hands of another or by natural causes, death can't be avoided. And when it comes, it comes for keeps. You may escape a time or two, but when the final curtain comes down, its all over.

My granny, Ne-Ne often said, "I ain't raring to go but I'm ready to go." My other grandma, Ma Dear laid out the details to her final wishes as she prepared to go on and leave us behind with 99 years of memories. They, like scores of others from their generations, had a certain peace about death. They waited their turn and there wasn't no kicking and screaming. They just transitioned from here to eternity.

Our generations are more used to burying those far younger than either of the matriarchs of the Bedford or Bolden clans. They just don't make them like they used to, I guess.

Long live Pabst Blue Ribbon and Colt .45 malt liquor!!

TRAVEL

We grew up traveling. My folks took us on vacation a couple of times a year. One, would be to go down south to see my dad's folks and the other would be somewhere else in the country. The old man always drove to where ever we were going. We would stay in the Howard Johnson's or Days Inn and it always had a pool!

We'd pull into a Stucky's and be wowed at all the stuff that they had inside the store. We were given a few bucks to buy some junk and stuff like little knick-knacks. My mother was notorious about those nasty ars peanut logs, yuck.

And here comes that but, that you knew was coming and here it is. But, as I got older, they started to leave me behind and I was cool with that, because, I was as my old man calls it, 'smelling my piss'.

Then I got to have the house all to myself and that was worth not going out of town in itself. No matter what me and the crew did, when my family got back home, the house was still standing and there wasn't any crime scene tape around it!

When my addiction took over, the only trips I was taking was one 'chasing the dragon'. A relentless assault on all the nurturing and sacrifices that was given to me. Then in 2009, I logged around 3000 miles of highway time and I been going ever since. MI, MN, MO, Springfield, WI, KY, TN, AR.

Hey, my mother still does my grocery shopping, ha!

LEISURE

Its so appropriate that she decided to leave this one to be last. I come from a very laid-back family. Not just the immediate Bedford/Bolden clan but our relatives as well. For the most part, when we got together it was a chillin' experience.

Not a lot of bickering, and yes, there were fist to cuffs every now and then. But the atmosphere overall was that of leisure. Who ever was hosting the get together always made it a no stress occasion. We knew the rules and we for the most part abided by them. Not too much was over the top. I guess that's why I'm the way that I am now. I like to just chill and relax watching tv or hitting the lake or taking in a baseball game.

I feel the most comfortable in a t-shirt and jeans more so than a suit and tie.

Last lil ditty about Billy regarding leisure.

Back in the day there were Leisure Suits and I had one. One day I was in that suit on a skate board and fell off. I was terrified because it was on a Sunday morning and going to church. When Gloria Geraldine Bedford saw the hole in that knee of the pants, I knew it was going to be 'curtains' for me. Instead of killing me, she made me wear the tattered suit to church. And my Ne-Ne finished me off by picking my hair with a fork!

Cyndi, top that!

THE F'N END!

Finally, we have reached the f'n (which stands for fargin) end of my bull-shiggitty. And I must admit it was a lot of fun and hope to be able to do it again sometime soon (that's called a hint).

So, without further ado, I want to take the time to thank Chucky, John Wick, The Equalizer, Freddy Krueger, Jason Vorhees, Leather Face, Predators, Aliens, Michael Myers, Ghost Rider, Jigsaw and the monster that started it all, Godzilla for slash, horror and gore at an unapparelled pace!

The United States of Billy: Ms. Chaka Khan, Denise Boutte, Morena Baccarin, Narrisa Knight, Pauley Purette, Terrie Vaughn, Tia Carrera, Rosie Perez, Kirstie Alley, Chelsea Spack, Ms. Tina Turner, Dana Brooke, Det. Lori Morgan, Det. Leslie Bradford, Bette Midler, Fran Dresher, Karen Jarrett, Debbie Harry, Erin Richards, J Woww, Andrea

Canning, Marcia Clark, Kerry Sayers, Loni Anderson, Aunt Fritzi, Pamela Anderson-Lee, A J Lee, Condelezza Rice, Caroline Rhea, The Iconics, Kim Fields, Beyonce, Lil Kim, Nikki Manaj, Eva Mendez Brett Somers, Fantasia, Cher, Jody Whatley, Jennie Mae Pollard, Jessica Lucas, Charlotte Flair, Naomi, Jennifer Hudson, Edie Falco, Rhianna, Jade, Drea de Matteo, Karen Gravano & the capital state of Lady Soul-Queen Aretha Franklin.

YOU SAY ONE THING AND I HEAR ANOTHER (WHERE IS MY RIGHT SHOE?)

By Cynthia Powell and Billy

As I reflect on this title You say one thing and I hear another.

It reminds me of how things are received differently between men and

women. Just how easy things could be taken out of context or just how

we look at things in our own ways.

Therefore, keeping the line of communication open in any relationship is very important.

INTIMACY

So, the very special question you must ask right out the gate: Are you single? Do you have a girlfriend? This is one thing you can't assume because the intimacy could come about first if you think that man was honest with you from the beginning and you find out later they weren't. If it is and honest person you want that intimacy with it can be a beautiful thing. Talking to each other and learning to understand each other can be an awesome experience. Physical intimacy can be shown by friendship, romantic love, sexual activity and platonic love.

Intimacy means having that feeling of being close to each other and belonging together. It is a close bond with each other that is formed through the experience and knowledge of each other. Opening your true self to your partner may not be easy at times because you may be worried what they might think about you and you don't want to open because you are afraid of being hurt. Not having good skills in developing intimacy can cause you to get close to quickly and make it hard to find boundaries and maintain a connection.

The fear of intimacy for a woman can be a real thing if she has been hurt on several occasions. It will make you gun shy because you keep opening yourself up and you keep getting hurt. This is frustrating and exhausting.

Remember intimacy is not just about being sexual. It is about sharing you true self with someone and opening up. You must be willing to be open and share to be intimate. You can't be guarded and want that intimacy and think you are going to get it when you're not willing to give it also.

If a woman typically requires closeness and intimacy before having a good sex experience does that mean they won't have sex before they feel intimate? No, it may often mean sex is not satisfying, even though you have an orgasm without close feelings. Some women feel *pressure to have sex before they are ready, and we think, this man doesn't love me for me. He only loves for what he can get from me. You might build up resentment against men in general. I believe women are more of a mystery to men than men are to women. Even though women are important to men, we live in our strange world of periods and babies and reeling emotions and even tears that you men can't or don't want to understand. Because men don't really talk about or express their feelings like they should it hard for them to figure ours out. Men think sex is a way to get closer to women and maybe a way to please them. They are usually wrong of course, it doesn't stop a man from thinking sex can make everything alright with his women. Like it is the cure for everything. If one or both partners need to know each other deeply, understood and accepted before they can be intimate any other way, it is important that the other partner(s) works to make that happen.*

Remember some couples today are struggling with something new to build based on real feelings of equality. There weren't many models of intimacy from our parents because they were too busy struggling and staying in survival mode. If you expect your partner to read your mind and understand what you need, then you must tell her or him. That means you must figure out yourself what you really need. You can't expect your partner to be sensitive and understand exactly how you feel about something unless you're able to talk about it to him or her and tell them how you feel in the first place. If you don't like and get what your partner is doing, ask why he or she is doing it and vice versa. Talk about it don't just assume what's going on. When your expressing your feelings about a certain situation and asking that your partner is honest with you in return is the way to discover truth in your relationship. Learning to listen not just hear is important. For, most women there are some basic truths when it comes to intimacy.

The funny thing is ours are pretty much the opposite of men's view of intimacy. Maybe if men could understand a little more their wife would be open to sex!

1. Emotional Beings

Even though men are visual, women can be more emotional. This means we as women are not as turned on by sight alone. While it may be nice to have a good-looking husband, but that is not where women's sexual desire rest. Women want to feel and be desired, cared for and loved. When a woman is emotionally taken care of it makes her feel comfortable and open to the idea of making love.

2. Love Language Needs

Women love to talk, and women love to be heard. A lot of time we love to listen too. Most men don't love to listen. But, if a man would take time to hear his wife (not fix her problem) it would only work out well for you.

If you want to take it a step further make sure you tell your wife how much you love and adore her.

3.   A Need for Love:
When a woman feels loved, we relax and open up to our men.
The arguments stop, the sex is on point and our feminine energy flows through our lives. Learn how to see through her words, moods and actions and see what the real cause is.

4. Partners helping each other with daily life:
The house chores even the cooking should be a shared duty. It may depend on work schedules or who has a job or not. It should be shared to make it easy on one another or pitch in and do it as a team. It is even more of a team effort when you have kids.

INTIMACY IS NOT PURELY PHYSICAL.

It's the act of connecting with someone so deeply, you feel like you can see into their soul.

ROMANCE

What is romance and what does it truly mean? Romance is an emotional attachment between people. When the endorphin's in the brain kick in and your emotions are on high, passion and exhilaration is on the rise. When you and your partner want to do things to show each other how much you love them.

Romance for us is a deep connection that they have to build with us. That is the ultimate form of romance. Now tell me who wouldn't enjoy a nice massage and then have a nice bubble bath waiting with candles all around after getting off work. Just so you can unwind and relax your mind before continuing with you day. How romantic is that? We women love romance and it's our mystic nature. There is something about intimate gestures of real love and true affection from that special one that gets our emotions fired up.

So, when a man takes the time to go out of his way to show you he is thinking of her just because. It will make you remember why you fell for that person in the first place. What does it mean to be romantic? Being romantic is what makes that love between two people so dog gone awesome! It is what draws the line between this relationship and all the others in each of your lives. Pay attention now men ha ha! When a woman asks you to be "more romantic," she is not asking you to spend more money, to do something over the top, or even to pretend to be old-fashion in some ways you're not. Being romantic means just going out of your way to show you truly care. It means showing her what you already know for yourself----that there is something about her that brings out a part of you that no one else knows or gets to see. For some of us women, practical gifts are not romantic at all. If we do like practical gifts, then you men need to look for gifts we can use or something with several uses.

The more functional the gift the better.
Remember romance is personal. So, to be that
romantic person, you must be personal and do
personal kinds of things. But being romantic
means that no matter how busy you are, you
will always make time —whatever time you can
spare to show her that your there for her and
you continue to be there. So, men when you do
this. This is the sexiest day ever. Being
romantic means, you would be willing to put
yourself in some not so comfortable positions
for her and yourself. Being romantic can also
mean showing her that even though you know
she is capable of taking care of herself, but you
want to take care of her in your own way as
well as her taking care of you right back. Now,
men do I need to give a few examples on what
to do to keep it romantic.

Here are a few:

1. Write her a love note and put them
   where she can find them in
   places she will least expect.

2. *Let her sleep in and you play with kids and make breakfast.*

3. *Putting on her favorite smell good even when there's no reason other than she loves how yummy you smell.*

4. *Making some eye contact with her and hold her hand while you talk over dinner.*

5. *Cook a wonderful meal for her at home.*

6. *Take a walk together and hold hands.*

7. *Have a slow dance together after putting the kids to bed*

8. *Make the first move (you know what I mean) wink! Wink!*

9. *Give her a nice foot, calf and ankle and neck rub.*

10. *Send her sweet text messages.*

Just to name a few. Women can always return the favor to their man but since I am speaking from my point of view.

A PERSON WHO FEELS APPRECIATED WILL ALWAYS DO MORE THEN WHAT IS EXPECTED.

TRUE LOVE

You might wonder what true love is about and what the signs of true love really is about. We need to understand that it is important to take things slow in your new relationship if you want it to be a success. Who doesn't want to have that special someone that they are truly in love with! A woman gives that special part of herself for that man to turn around and devastate her by telling her he no longer loves her. We can accept that special love doesn't happen instantly; it is a gradual process. It grows after you've gone through some ups and downs, when you have laughed together, cried together and suffered together. True love does take time to grow. We, as women we show our emotions in different ways then men do, and when we fall in love, we show a type of behavior that makes it obvious how we feel. Only if you know what to look for. That is why the guys who know you love them run, because they figured it out. Men should be honest with women up front to let them know if they want the same thing. It brings to my mind the word "unconditional" no expectations or limitations set. But to love with unconditional love is difficult and us humans aren't good at it. True love does love without trying to make another person change. True love means you must put the other persons need equal to, or before your own. When you are in love with a person (just my thought) you are free to really be yourself without worrying about being judged and critical of you. So, in my opinion love is feeling that the other person totally loves and accepts you for who you are and vice versa.

True Love is when two people touch each other 'soul.

True Love is honesty and trust.

True Love is helping one another.

True Love is mutual respect.

True Love means that differences can be worked through.

True Love is reaching your dreams together.

True Love is the connection of two hearts.

BLACK LOVE (Men and Women)

What can say about Black Love. Black Love is beautiful! Each time something gets thrown at it, it only gets better. Black Love shouldn't exist in America at all in any form. Everything in our history was done to prevent it. The structure of slavery was that love and other ideals, would not develop. Families were separated from each other time and time again. Father and mothers were killed, men, women and children were raped. Marriage was forbidden amongst blacks only if it was sponsored by a white person, even after that it was only in certain states. White supremacy has tried to kill the spirit of black love, because it was threat to oppression. White supremist did their best to make it a figment of our imagination. For many people, it still is the attack on black love. I think it had a two-sided possibility though. As a matter of fact, it made black love even stronger in other forms. We love really hard, family and others, because our spirit knows what it is like not to have it.

We had to create ways to show our children that they were loved during slavery. Black love at some point developed on a spiritual level because we didn't have the chance to love in person. The ideal of black love was the opposite of how America viewed black than, and even how they do now. They tried to destroy us through slavery, but black love persisted. My sister's is it true a good (black) man is hard to find? You ladies that are single have a real good answer to that question for me. My ears are burning HA HA! Even though dating is hard for lots of people but for black women in the United States, it can be awful. For one thing, we're expected to stand up to white beauty standard. Another thing is there are so many racist stereotypes: that we are angry, lazy, overbearing just to name a few. Oh yeah, right and we don't have a good since of humor at times. the stereotyping and expectations do a couple of things. One they can limit the number of people who are interested in being with black women. Two, they create situations where we as black women, try really hard not to fit in these categories. Almost makes you not want to do the dating thing "right". If that is not enough black women have to contend with some serious stereotypes about black men. You will never understand the hard experience watching the black man demean and try to destroy our self-esteem and the sanctity of Black women while praising women of other races. This can be so hurtful. You must understand Black brothers that us Black women may appear to be totally upset but did you ever consider we might be scared. Maybe we make it seem like were hard on the outside, but we put that block up to protect our world that is constantly being judged. So, remember the next time you make a smart comment about us that will contribute to our attitude so try saying" thank you "sometimes. Don't forget without the Black woman, there would be no you. We should be loved and cherished and treated with the utmost respect. As a black power couple, *you should nurture, love and respect one another and always keep your line of communication open. My feelings on this subject truly comes down to, Men if you find you a Black Queen hold on to her and hold her in high esteem. Women if you find your Black King hold him tight. You both love each other like you want to be loved.*

Never Give Up on Black Love!

DATING

What can I say to women about dating life. It can be good, and it can have it challenges for sure. Is it that men don't want to put the work into dating or what. Some men be a little lazy when it comes to relationships. Why do black men think black women are difficult to deal with? Who saying we are? Are they just guessing, or do they know firsthand. Have you tried to get to know us when we are dating to see what we are about. We seem to be judged based on some hard stereotypes rather than being assed as an individual. Let's keep it real when a black woman points something out, it is taken way out of proportion and we can be labeled full of drama. When someone with less melanin does it, it is totally accepted with open arms. If black women are desired, we must deal with other biases. Your color while dating always seems to find it way around. Our men swear that they love them some black women, but that love sometimes too comes with filters like ones on Facebook. So Black

Women do you feel invisible when you're out at single's events. Do you feel like the black men are interested and they overlook you? Do black women feel the black men that notice them don't live up to their expectations?

What is wrong with dating a strong black woman. we are not trying to be the man in the relationship. She is hopeful and eager to meet and build with a life partner. Maybe sometimes we need to do somethings on our own. That doesn't mean that a man still can't be a man. It means that like you, we want to tap into our strength. If we can do this at times, we will be vulnerable with you than you could ever dream of. You need to support our purpose and passion. What makes us such strong Black woman is our confidence and the drive to go after what we want in life. We do not always have superhuman strength. We have fears, worries, anxieties and concerns that others have. That's where you come in men.

You serve as our inspiration as we travel on our journey to become our higher selves. So, it okay to be a genuine, supportive and loving partner that we need. If you are going to date us strong Black women, remember we are passionate, sensual and delicate. As women no matter how, head strong we can be, we still desire to turn over our power to some degree. We can be smart and resourceful, so it is hard to put something over on us. Do us a favor and be as honest about your intentions as possible. I am sure everyone has their likes and dislikes but when most of those men seem to want women who don't look like you. Maybe it's time to change up the dating game a bit. The cure for being invisible is to get visible. You can't have any control over someone else's desires and interests. You can only let your light shine bright! I think to you should meet each person and get to know them on and individual basis. don't judge on site get to know the person before you pass judgement. No disrespect to any other races but I can only speak from my point of view. I want to ask my Sister's a question how you felt when the person you were dating had been in a relationship with another race before dating you did it make you feel some type of way, like why did he choose me, or did you feel like you had to live up to a certain image? Maybe these are some of the thoughts that might go through your head. One thing I do know is you must keep the line of communication open and be, honest with one another. There is nothing more devastating than to find out what you thought was true wasn't because that person didn't have the decency to be honest. Instead they were a coward instead.

"NOT COOL AT ALL!" BE YOURSELF, IT IS THERE LOSS THAT THEY ARE MISSING OUT ON AND AMAZING PERSON!

TO MAKE BETTER CHOICES WHEN IT COMES TO DATING

YOU HAVE TO ACCEPT THE FACT THAT YOU CAN INDEED

CHOOSE WHOM YOU FALL FOR. ITS UNDERSTAND THAT IN

WHOMEVER YOU INVEST YOUR TIME AND ENERGY INTO YOU WILL DEVELOP FEELINGS FOR. ITS ALSO

UNDERSTANDING THAT YOU SHOULD APPLY WISDOM

RATHER THAN GOING WITH THE EMOTION FLOW,

BECAUSE THAT'S HOW TOO MANY PEOPLE HAVE FALLEN

FOR THOSE THEY SHOULDN'T HAVE, AND DROWNED

THEMSELVES IN TERRIBLE RELATIONSHIPS.

TOILET PAPER

Don't Forget to Carry Toilet Paper with You Everywhere! Nothing is more disturbing then to have to go to the bathroom bad and you're out somewhere and go into the stall and there is no toilet paper in there. I don't care which way my toilet paper rolls as long as I can get to it. I heard there actually is a proper way for it to roll and that is the "over" position go figure. I have walked into the women's bathroom and there was toilet paper all over the floor. I guess it was just because they were covering the seat, so they could use it. I suppose whatever paper slides on the floor they just let it. Then you must worry about it sticking to the bottom of your shoes if the floor is wet. I have gone as far as putting a small bottle of disinfectant in my purse sprayed the toilet and wiped it off with toilet paper. Sometimes there can be and emergency and hovering over won't do. Your stomach is not quite right. Too much information huh!

I can also think of a few past uses for toilet paper. Do some of you remember as a teenager stuffing your bra ha trying to make you have something you knew you never would and some regretting they rushed that process. And the not so fun tp'ing when some kids played a prank and hung toilet paper on trees and threw all over the yard. Oh yeah, the making spit wads. Who came up with this stuff. Excuse me I was reminiscing and having a throwback moment.

Bathrooms (His and Hers)

My ultimate ideal of co-habituating bathrooms would be a sink, toilet, spa tub and shower. Then there is a mirrored area that you could come out to, so you can check out how you look as it spins so you can see every angle well maybe us women would only appreciate that one. Then you could worry about cleaning your own bathroom and what you leave on the sink and not worried about the toilet seat being up and how much toilet paper you use and how long you stay in there so many perks for having your own bathroom instead of using the same one. When you move in with that special someone, it is only natural for you to want to put your own mark on a place, but remember you have another person's flair and tastes to consider too. The bathroom is a space that families sometime may have to share. When it just two people the bathroom becomes a place to relax- a place to release the stress of the day.

For men the plus side of his bathroom are a wonderful reason and some benefits to consider having his and her separate bathrooms:

Amounts of products you use

Length of primping time

Different schedules

Type of bathroom situations

Having separate bathrooms can help couples with clashing personalities and help establish a sense of space.

The bathroom can be a functional room that serves basic essentials:

Shaving

Washing

"Taking care of your personal business"

No need for any bright or fancy colors. Again, I say the best spot is he can

be responsible for his own cleaning "yay"

For Her

It is simple, his and hers bathrooms can be your family therapist. We as women have a different relationship with her bathroom then a man would. For us it is a place to un wind in the tub or to escape for the stress of the day.

Having separate bathrooms can help couples understand how to get along in the same home.

So, if it is possible for you to have separate bathrooms I say go for it!

Divorce

Divorce is never easy. It can make you feel like you have failed and a piece of you is missing especially when you have been with this person for years the time invested and the love you shared with one another. It can be a tough adjustment on both parties immediately after the marriage is officially over. You should be aware of the possible consequences of divorce, and to have a real view of the future. Only in the movies and not real life will a handsome, rich, eligible man going to appear out of the blue and give us divorced women everything we ever dreamed of. For real, women normally suffer the most after a divorce. Their emotional well-being as well as their quality of life. We as women suffer financially after divorce, some women were housewives and didn't have to work because that husband had a good job so, this and be devastating for someone who goes through a divorce and doesn't have a job skill to support themselves. also, if the women are the only caregiver to the children without the husband's salary, she will not have enough money to cover her bills and the household expenses. We woman feel unhappy, hurt and lonely. Even if it was your choice to end the marriage anyway. You may have wounds from this broken relationship for a long time. The stress and strain of and unhappy marriage maybe be replaced by different kind of worries. One is not being able to trust any man again. and trying to find that prince charming and the darn fear of being rejected repeatedly. Despite the negative effects on us as women, there are many cases that lead to healthier and happier lives. Some of us woman may need to seek some professional help to get over our unhealthy relationship and breakdown of a marriage especially if we have been a victim of an abusive relationship. I have heard people say you should go to church and go to your pastor and get counseling, but somethings the pastor isn't equipped to handle certain situations. For divorce to have a chance to have a positive affect than a negative one, we must try to make the most of the chance to change our lives for the better. For the first few years after a divorce can be a crucial time for some personal growth and some more personal life choices. It is a time to working making your life better. You have a few decisions to make after a divorce, from how to be able to increase your income, where you're going to live. These become very important. A divorce can be the hardest thing a woman has to face. It can cause so many life-threatening issues. Also, when dealing with the children from your union you don't want to bad mouth one another or argue and fight in front of them. They go through changes from a divorce just like you do. This can be such a difficult time you must keep your temper under wraps as much as you can. Keep in mind the kids aren't getting a divorce you are. The children will still continue to have a relationship with the other parent. No matter how you two might feel about each other don't discourage their parent and child relationship. There are a few things that can cause marriage breakdown like infidelity, abuse, addiction, lack of communication and falling out of love. Differences in religion and politics. Even the lack of education on one or both people parts can also be a factor in divorce. Some divorce situations can be very hard to get out and get through also. It does take time to recovery from it allow yourself to do that for your mental and physical health. Be kind and loving to yourself. It can be a tuff journey at times, but you can get through it one day one step at a time. Stay prayed up!

Jezebel

Woo wee let's talk about that Jezebel sprit it is something else. Who was jezebel? According to the bible Jezebel was described in the book of kings as a queen and she was the daughter of Ithobaal I of Sidon and wife of Ahab, King of Israel. The Book of Kings in the Hebrew bible says Jezebel caused her husband King Ahab to abandon the worship of Yahweh and encouraged him to start worshipping the deity's Baal and Asherah instead. Jezebel talked evil of and persecuted the prophets of Yahweh and made up evidence of blasphemy against and innocent landowner who didn't want to sell his property to King Ahab, causing him to be put to death. For this transgression against God and the people of Israel. Jezebel met a horrible death. She was thrown out the window by members of her own court and the flesh of her corpse was eaten by stray dogs.

In this bible story Jezebel becomes associated with some false prophets. From the description in the bible, she dressed well and wore make-up. This led to the association of the using of cosmetics with prostitutes. How do the "Jezebel sprit" apply today? The Jezebel sprit isn't just one spirit like Satan is. There is one kind of evil spirit in the Satan's kingdom. There is only one devil; and one Satan, but there are so many spirits that would be considered a Jezebel spirit type, as they all have similar type of personality and specific ways in which they like to operate. The reason a lot of deliverance ministers have come to use these words to coin the phrase "jezebel spirit", because of its personality and the way it operates. Some examples, of the function of names of demons could be spirits of anger, lust, murder, etc. The spirit of anger will get a person to act out in fits of rage and anger. The spirit of murder will try to get someone to commit cold- bloodied murder. Also, the spirit of lust will try to get a person to commit fornication or adultery. A Jezebel spirit in a woman won't submit to a man, if she does she will only pretend to get her way. Her submission has conditions. A jezebel thinks that he or she can get any man or woman they want, even if that person is with someone already. This is because Jezebel finds the fun in destroying relationships and feels empowered by knowing that another woman's man or another man's women is paying them attention. Do not get close to a person with a Jezebel spirit because they would use your secrets against you in the future. Even when you are in a happy and loving relationship, of which God chose you and your partner. Know Jezebel will be after you. It is important that you and your significant discuss having boundaries Sometimes, when you come across a Jezebel spirit, it can be something quite different. Remember in the bible Matthew 12:43 tells us there are different levels of wickedness in Satan's kingdom. And in the level of wickedness some demons are eviler than others. Self -exalting and self-promoting is alive and well in the church today. Many want the recognition but no the brokenness; the honor not the humility; to be in the limelight but not the loneliness. The pulpit can be affected: altering life giving preaching cost the preacher much, death to his soul. This Jezebel spirit has been responsible for not just tearing down pastors, churches, and several Christian ministries, but it can also be responsible for breaking up marriages, companies, friendships, and getting people to do awful things like committing murders and suicides. Don't be seduced by the Jezebels that surrounds you today----turn to the Most High. Be watchful and Pray!

Celibacy

You are fearfully and wonderfully made and there is nothing wrong with saving yourself, for what you pray for to be the right one. There are so many more single women in the United States than there are married ones. There are some women that go out on dates, and meeting someone on the on-line dating sites. But there are some of them who aren't. Some women are voluntarily celibate, but not for religious reasons. Also, with so many STDs around many people shy away from casual sexual encounters. You should be using condoms between all lovers, even in a relationship, until at some point it becomes a monogamous is decided upon. Even with all of that, there are possible risk and mistakes that could happen. Sometimes I feel when you are in what you hope is a monogamous relationship. The person you're with is honest with you and not trying to lie to you just to sleep with or in a marriage that shouldn't be cheating on you. They should be communicating with one another and making sure they keep their marriage tight and right, so the bond can't be broken. Some people choose to be celibate after a bad breakup because they are emotionally exhausted from the break-up and it seems like the right time to step away and focus on yourself. Some choose to be celibate until marriage and gives you a chance to explore being on your own. Not only being single, but independent by choice. Celibacy can be a choice because of your religious beliefs. The best part is not worry about getting pregnant or any sexual transmitted diseases. It can also help you in other ways as well. Until you meet that special person to spend your life with. it can teach you how to have a great deal of patience. The hardest part is staying celibate. You may feel a certain way at the start ---very strong-minded and motivated—but then a couple of months roll by and them hormones rise- up and kick in OH BOY! Keep in mind your happiness comes from within. Being celibate can help you *to have more self -appreciation and a lot more love for yourself.*

House Chores

Let's, talk house chores, I think it should be a joint venture where the situations apply. The women shouldn't do all the chores. Women are in the work force as much as the men. Who does what and how do you figure it out? And what does it mean to do your equal share and live in harmony. The truth is a lot of house chores will mean something different for every relationship because of the expectations of what each partner should be doing. That could be a good thing if a couple have an equal contribution with chores this could only enhance a couple's relationship because nobody is stressed out about who didn't do what or who should do what. It could make for the possibility of couples having more frequent sex and getting along better, because they agreed on the housework being evenly distributed. Maybe the amount of housework would mean something different to every relationship because of the expectations of what each partner should do. I know men may still think of us as nurtures, caregivers, house hold caretakers, givers of life, etcetera. So maybe naturally man think women should cook, clean and do it all. Even when there out in the work force. I think it is something that you be talked about and compromised on at some point to make the household and life run smoothly.

Loud Music

When is the last time you turned your radio up while saying oh man that's my jam ha ha. I remember sitting on the top of speaker at concerts back in the day A no no! Maybe you don't listen to it loud all the time, but you have at some point. The youth these days put a lot of louder bass and offensive words to their music. It can be disturbingly loud to others around them. I wish the young people could understand that constant exposure could result in hearing loss over time. Playing loud music can also, be considered rude by society and other people too. Because some people don't take well to loud music. They think it is very disrespectful. They may appreciate the loud music more in a concert or dance club atmosphere. I think listening to it and being considerate of others around you is the key.

Sometimes That Loud Music is the Only Medicine the Heart and Soul

Mr. Fix It

Ladies, have you had that husband or boyfriend that is not mechanically inclined. They are good at other things around the home but not that. My opinion on that is if they can't fix anything, hopefully they have a telephone book full of reliable people that can be called when problems arise. That helps a lot! Now there is that other end of the coin if the man is mechanically inclined he offers to do it to make her feel better. Men may get a little confused if we don't appreciate their gesture of love and trying to help. Maybe no matter how many times we tell them they're not listening, and they don't get it and keep doing the same thing over. Maybe our man feel we are trying to change them or tell them what to do. We love our men and want to help them improve the way they do somethings. We feel in some way we are nurturing them, while they might feel we are controlling them. I came to my own understanding. A man can feel offended when a woman offers her advice when he is trying to fix things and our men think we don't trust his ability to do it himself. Maybe we don't get why you're so sensitive about it. We women are just happy you love us enough to want to fix things around the house. So maybe I get now why when we offer to help you. It may make you feel like we think you can't accomplish it. When we know this isn't true. Or our timing may not be the best. Hopefully we can communicate through this process without any difficulty. Praying never hurts along with it either in some cases HA HA!

Gas

Sorry to break it to you gas is a natural thing
and it can happen when you least expect it. It
can be embarrassing at times. What I can tell
if you tell someone to stay where you are and
not to follow you when you are gassy they are
strictly on their own. You gave them fair
warning. There are also people who are
pranksters and they think farting on you is
funny. Sometimes, you can have some gas that
when you release it more than just gas comes
out. It is not a good feeling at all. Also, as you
get younger those milk and cheese products
don't react to your body well and cause you
gas. So, can some medications you take. There
are also silent and deadly gas. Some of you
know what I am referring too. You can also
become gassy if you eat too quickly. Maybe a
new food you try doesn't agree with your
system. If you swallow a lot of air. It can

happen too. If you're on a new diet and changing the way you eat. It is one of those things that can happen to you when you least expect it. Enough on this subject for me.

Shopping

What women doesn't love shopping. It can be wonderful retail therapy. My least favorite for me is window shopping. Don't care for that some women can do that. New clothes can change your whole mood and the way you look at yourself. There are also some men who like to shop as much as women. I don't think there is anything wrong with it. At least they care about the way they look. When I walk into the store I must have a conversation with myself. Those shoes are on sale! Do I really need those it's not as if I don't have enough already? I think shopping for us women is just like sports is for men. We love it and are passionate about all in one. I love a good bargain when I decide to go out shopping that is what I am looking for. I enjoy taking my time looking. Not being rushed if I am doing it that way I don't end up getting something I really like. I end up with some item I settled on. if I have a rough day going shopping works for me and cheers me up. I try to make sure

when I am shopping for something I have a
budget in mind when I go so I don't over
spend. Also, shopping can become a
replacement of something that may be lacking
in your life and that is our way of coping with
things sometimes. Not always a good thing but
it can be a real thing. I remember when my
girls were at that age where we could wear the
same clothes. I would hide my purchases from
them in the trunk of the car and bring them in
and put them in the back of the closet.
Thinking for sure they were hidden from them.
To see them wearing some of my purchases. Oh
boy that was a challenge. As well as wearing
my perfume earrings etc. What an adventure
that was. We go thru this when you have
daughters. What women doesn't want to look
her best. If you look good you feel good!

Listening

This subject for me isn't an easy one for me. There were so many times when I wasn't heard, and I was in a dark place on my journey. I always hoped I made the right decision even when I wanted someone to listen and give me some good advice to help me with through my difficult time then. It helped me to decide to listen to others more. I decided to become a life coach and give people the same opportunity I missed out on. I wanted to help people on their journeys. Been their done that and was a member of that club. I believe that was the gift the Most High gave me to help others. Let me make it clear I am not blaming anyone that I came to when I needed someone to listen. People have their own things going on in their life, so I blame no one. Maybe at times I just wanted someone to listen to me period.

When you're dealing with someone else in your life it is important to hear each other out and keep the line of communications open. I realized listening is not the same as hearing. When you are listening, you must pay attention not only to the story but how it's being told, the voice as well as language usage and pay attention to someone body language. I had to learn when I listening to someone I pay close attention to verbal and non-verbal messages. I think when somebody is listening to you. If there is something they don't understand. They need to ask questions to make sure, they fully understand. People don't always need advice. Sometimes all they really need is a hand to hold, and ear to listen, and a heart to understand them.

Why do I keep trying?

I can say from a business owner point of view.
I would keep trying different things for it to
flourish. I would keep trying from a business
standpoint. Who doesn't want to be successful
in the business world. I would try repeatedly
to reach what I want to my key to success. I
can say it has its up and down moments and it
can get you a little down. It can be lonely at
the top. if there is a slow period. When you
come up with ideals and want to put them
together and people don't seem to support you.
That helps me push even harder even when I
am not sure how it was going to go. If I am
working on ideals and plans it is always on a
good path. It's when you stop doing anything
and you know longer pursue any ideals is when
you lose interest and give up. Let's, talk about
should I keep trying when it comes to a
relationship. You have feelings and fall in love
with them. You must remember with any
relationship you're in you must keep your line
of communication open. If you no longer have

that it won't work, and you might as well give-up. For me I say it depends on the person I am dealing with. How they act and what kind of person they are. What they have done? It would help me make my decision on whether I would continue to try or not. We do have to be patient with ourselves to understand even if we take a few steps back. It is not the end of the world

Grooming

As a woman, grooming can be a high maintenance routine at times. All the plucking, tweezing, exfoliating and shaving all in the name of grooming, sometimes it can be exhausting. You must worry about your hair, nails, feet, skin, make-up etc. you have to make sure you hair is on point and take good care of your teeth and your breathe smells fresh. It turns into a pampering session which is not a bad ideal. You go get a pedicure and manicure a massage. Not only do these things make you feel good. They can lift you spirits. I also must talk about hair styles just trying to find something that's flattering. Whether your hair is natural, or it has weave in it. It can be a challenge to come up with something. Trying to find make-up to enhance your beauty. I like going as natural as I can unless it is some special event.

You must worry about getting make-up on your clothes. Also, so I feel staying as close as you can to a natural look is the most beautiful. I think grooming is important for your physical and mental outlook. Let me get little personal and talk about the public area! This is very important to our personal hygiene women. if you're going natural there is nothing you need to do but keep it fresh and clean. You can trim or shape if you feel the need too. Some of us shave it all off. Your choice! Even though I am sure that hair grow they're for a reason. No judgement just saying. You can really do as you please. Pubic hair is there to cushion and to protect the skin around your genitals. It is also part of hygiene, trapping bacteria and dirt and stopping it from entering the vagina opening. This is your choice bare or hair, we women are beautiful regardless. It means you love you enough to care about how you look.

Sex

As a woman I find sex to be the deepest form of love and connection. We are sexual beings. We woman have the capacity for powerful and pleasurable multiple orgasms. I believe for us woman sex begins in the mind. For us we fantasize, remember and imagine hot sex which put us on the road to heating up. I feel we want to be desired. When we have busy lives our sex life can be delayed because of the day we had, maybe were in some pain. Romance and seduction play a big part in sex. Sex, hanging out, talking, working together keeping the home running smoothly, being appreciated, celebrating the holidays may comprise your love for us women. I think we realize our partners need for sex and we want to meet that need for him. If you receive the warmth and passion from that partner, it can be beautiful expression of love. It is a mood motivator. Even if sex doesn't end with an orgasm. We women want to feel desired and loved and appreciated too. I think we should be able to talk to each other about our needs and desires openly without judgement and vice versa. They shouldn't always make the result of that all about them each time. Let's talk about that subject a lot of us may not want to talk about masturbation. I think it is totally healthy and normal. For sure you won't get HIV or any STDS and you won't get hurt emotionally be a partner so many wins. It can also get to the point that most people know that masturbation can be normal and common.... even if they don't want to admit to it. Even some of us may be embarrassed about masturbating. You might feel a shame and dirty about doing it. Just because you partner masturbates (or they think they want to masturbate) ...it doesn't mean you don't satisfy them or that you're not attracted to them. You deserve to feel comfortable exploring your own body in the privacy of your own space. Adult sex toys have played a part in the sex lives of many adults. I don't think it's a bad thing sometime also because it could possibly enhance that sexual experience. That person may not be able to keep up with their partner sometimes or they have a difficult time having and orgasm. So, I think married couples should discuss these things openly with one another without judgement.

Friendship

Ladies I know your friendship with your girlfriends are very important to you. They are to me too! You can talk to them about some deeper things in your life. It doesn't matter the distant or time between me and my real good friends. Once we are friends. We are always friends. I don't care if it is has been years since we seen each other. The trust and love I have for them never changes. If feels like a sisterhood or family with them. We have watched each other's children, ate dinner sometime together and shared some sense of intimacy that comes from the bond of sisterhood. I have learned things from my friends. We have taken care of each other and we can always count on each other. We share a special bond when we are together. We encourage and support one another and help each other through some of life's ups and downs. Being able to count on your friends who love you, when you're going through rough times and make things easier to bear.

Our friends take an interest into what happens in your and they accept you for who you are. They have a listening ear for you when you need it. Just recently going on a girls trip with some of my girlfriend's was awesome and relaxing. Having a good friend is like a beautiful jewel, treasure it!

Loyalty

I must ask do you think you can tell how loyal a person is? Sometimes you don't know the extent of a person's loyalty until it is challenged. This is one I struggled with at times. I hope they are loyal, but I do keep my guard up. Loyalty is an important quality in a close relationship. Loyalty is important to the success and stability of a long-lasting relationship. Being loyal is being respectful of your partners weakness and helping them compensate without them knowing for their weakness. Not embarrassing them in public or private and keeping all their secrets. You shouldn't share things people tell you in confidence. Also, being loyal you should keep your word and be trustworthy. Whether it is your friendship, family, work, business. Loyalty comes from specific characteristics. Just because someone is a neighbor, friend, member of the family. It doesn't mean they

will be loyal. You always hope for this to be
true, but loyalty must be earned. I try to keep
in mind that we are all a work in progress. We
all must strive to do better in this area. I feel
it's not right to judge someone for not having
the ability to be loyal. I believe friendship and
loyalty run hand in hand. I think in any
relationship you should have loyalty as well as
love and respect. I feel as partners you should
be loyal to one another and you should be
mature enough to be in a relationship to begin
with. Life has taught me that you can't
control peoples loyalty. No matter how good
you can be to them, doesn't mean they will
return the favor. No matter how important
they are to you, doesn't mean they value you
the same way. Sometimes the people you have
love for the most, can turn out to be the people
you trust the least.

Emotions

Your emotions are important to your ability to cope with the task of your daily life. When we are feeling good it is easy to blow off the most burdensome task. But when you are feeling miserable that can be your hardest job ever. Emotions affect our interactions with others. You know we can be in a certain kind of mood and it can affect how were treated. I think when it comes to emotions we have to be able not to not let a person's negative energy creep in. Getting angry can really throw your energy off. Challenging your thoughts and things you believe about yourself can change your emotional reactions. Emotions cause you to survive and thrive. Each emotion has a purpose in your daily life. I have tried meditation and saying a positive mantra to keep my emotion sin check. I try to keep in my I can only do something about the things I can do something about. Other things that are out of my control, I can't do anything about them at all. If we don't get a handle on our emotions, then our emotions will manage us. This takes some practice to master. Just be patient with yourself it will get better.

Life Style

When we live on our own life terms. We have our own beliefs and the ways we choose to live our life. Life style can mean different things to different people. Our lifestyle is the way we work and relax. Our self-image, the way we see ourselves and the way we believe we are seen by others. The way we choose to live should make us happy. If it doesn't it is time for some lifestyle changes. I have tried some new changes in my life although they can be a bit scary and exciting all at the same time. Everything worked out fine when it was all said and done. There is no substitute for good mental health when you are struggling with some behavior health issue. Your lifestyle really affects how you feel and you can become your own best mental health by taking some steps toward a healthy lifestyle. We all have tried new foods, maybe vegan lifestyle. Trying new exercise regium. Try making a bucket list. Put some things on it you would like to try. You might be pleasantly surprised at just how adventurous you can be. I made myself a bucket list I have added a few more to it recently. Hoping this will give me a continued happy and healthy lifestyle.

Insurance

We women need affordable and comprehensive healthcare access. This has been important political issue for a few years. We are at a higher risk whether were underinsured and uninsured because usually we are covered through that working spouses employee plan. Even though concerns for us go much further than uninsured. Even when we have insurance it is still uncertain as to the coverage, higher out of pocket costs even discrimination based on gender. Insurers justify charging more for women because healthcare issues are more complex then men's. Most insurance companies see dollar signs when it comes to our coverage. It doesn't mean that we still won't run into some roadblocks to full health insurance. We are less likely than our men counter parts to be covered by our employees. I also want to mention why women need life insurance as well. Over the years our roles have changed a bit. There are more women who are the breadwinner of their household, as well as a stay at home mom and single parent working that 9 to 5 or anything in between, we all need life insurance more than ever. Having to buy life insurance is not fun at all. Who wants to plan for death? Nobody does! When we should be busy living life to its fullest.

Finance

We all need to take control of our money, although is important for women over there 50s. Us women live longer than men for the most part. Many wives outlive their husbands and at some point, manage their finances. We still make less money than men, so we must make our money work even harder. You shouldn't be shy at all about asking for help with your finances. Keep in mind as women we tend to put others needs first, or maybe some of us believe we can rely on a husband. But the reality is we need to take care of ourselves.

Investing

When it comes to investing our money, we tend to hold on to it tight because we have worked so hard for it. Our financial freedom can't happen if you don't have positive cash flow. I don't think we are as aggressive as men when it comes to this subject. Some of the reasons for this could be lower earnings from receiving a smaller paycheck and because of it we try not to lose the little we have already. It seems to me we live longer than men, and we are likely to have higher healthcare costs. Some of these costs can be medicine, hospitalization, surgery, long-term care. If you invest in bonds it could lead to greater long-term life returns, then investing in bonds. Maybe between our genders, the female investor outshine the men. We women are more cautious about taking risk and we worry more about our losses. Men are more on the competitive side and we are all about the goal. If you focus on the goal that is *ideal, it forces you to consider some of your personal needs instead of some random measure of success. It is about individual goals. A rule of thumb is the more time your money can work in your behalf the higher the risk. Remember risk is always present when it comes to your finances. Sometimes you may make a not so good decision. But, knowing when and what to sell is as important as knowing what to buy. You must be willing to let your money work for you.*

Sports

I love me some sports football, basketball etc. Who said we can't love some sports just as much as men. We are big fans of sports and play sports as well. Women who love and are fans of sports are not rare. Why do you men think we require a quiz to prove our loyalty to sports. Women are used to having their opinion overlooked on the assumption of being uninformed. I know this is a man's world(sports) and typically being a sports fan is strictly a man thing, not necessarily! Women can be just as passionate about sports as men. What is wrong with us women liking some so called "man stuff". So, what if I am a woman and a sports fan ha! Maybe men are partiality shocked if we do. In some cases, maybe we are the one dragging them to a game and the man isn't interested that happens you know. Even thinking liking sports makes you masculine plus, women equals butch= lover of ladies (not true). Men would you be so barking up the wrong tree. Or on the opposite end of the coin your husband or boyfriend thinks you're the greatest. He might even think he hit the mother lode your beautiful, smart, fun to be with, have a beautiful sense of humor, ambitious. All rolled into one. We can also know as much as men about what going on at the game. We are not only looking at the game because the guys have on tight uniforms. Just think you get wife or girlfriend who loves the game as much as you and can understand you watching Sunday night and Monday night football. Can make for a great date night. Something else you can do together to keep you relationship interesting.

Chivalry

Chivalry is what I would consider doing for the people I love and even friends I care for. It's just another name for treating people in my life, including strangers kindly and with some respect. Chivalry is about matters, and just being polite. At one time men would hold doors open for ladies, even if they were not dating. It was just such a polite thing to do. I think chivalry still exist although you don't see it often. Maybe men feel women are more independent, so they just feel the need to treat them equal. Chivalry can be a two-way street. You know like doing little special things for one another. showing how much, you care and love each other. It is nice to surprise each out like that. Keeps some excitement in your relationship. Chivalry calls the men to honor their. women and serve as their helpmates. This means the natural order of things. Men should honor women first as individuals, but

nurturers of life. There are not so good men
that commit violence against women, or treat
them with disrespect, it is a sin against nature.
Love relationships provide the place where
virtues of chivalry are tested to the fullest. You
sometimes in our relationships the appreciation
we have for each other does sometime go
unnoticed and gets taken for granted. Chivalry
also helps reinforce the expression of affections
and feelings that men have for their partner.
Chivalry is still alive and well for both men
and women and its continued practice helps
bring you together as a couple in a more
intimate and respectful way. Chivalry never
died. Just the gentleman in most men did.
Being male is a matter of birth. Being a man is
a matter of age, but being a gentleman is a
matter of choice.

Fear

However independent you may find yourself to be, there might be some truth to the saying "always needing a man." Let me see if I can explain what I mean by this. If you are single and your living alone. Come home to the house by yourself can be interesting because you have to pay attention to your surroundings. I had one of my friends tell me one time she was getting in her car early one morning and someone tried to rob them. See screamed she said and they ran away. She was truly blessed that everything turned out ok and she wasn't hurt. To any women who have experienced anything like or worse I am sorry, and it is too bad we don't have a world where you can take a late walk or just to get to your job safely without feeling threatened. I don't want this to ruin the good standing of all men, but I want you to be aware of what is happening out there in this big world. For sure we should appreciate those people in our life who are good to you, both men and women. Also, we have the fear of loneliness. Our reality is we are often afraid of our unavailability and independence. We may be able to go without relationships for a certain period of time. Until we realize we don't want to spend the rest of our lives like this, and we start looking for a partner. There are many of us 40 and 50 somethings that are ready to get married to a compatible man just not to be alone. Some time we can get overwhelmed by that fear of loneliness and we are ready to let our guard down and let that special person in. Or that fear of that one day soon we can't recognize that reflection in the mirror- were starting to age gracefully. When we start to get older no beautiful clothes or make up will work. even though understand this can be a fear of a women of any age. You always want that husband or boyfriend who could eventually be husband material. You hope they love you for you, that is why there with you in the first place. So, none of these feels are never a concern. They should be showing you attention and admiration, giving you compliments, even saying nice things if it will help you stop thinking about it. We have had that fear of not want to live in poverty and being able to make a good life for ourselves. We love being comfortable and cozy and our material welfare much more than men do. That is why we blame them for their mercenary spirit. But it comes from their fear of poverty. We do have things we want sometimes. So, either we want a man to provide for us or we do our best to provide for ourselves. This is where our careers come from. You hope your husband or future husband material can eliminate this fear for you. We need to see that you have good money managing skills, so we feel easy about planning a future with you without any fears. Just to name a few. Try not to feed you're your *fears. Try your best to let your faith be bigger than your fear.*

Death

Let's talk a little about death. This is never an easy subject to speak about. Most people think that death is the cessation of the connection between the body and mind. People believe that death occurs when the heart stops beating, but that doesn't mean that the person died, because the subtle mind still remains in the body. This is a little on the physical view of death. When this conversation is presented it isn't easy especially if aging parents bring that topic. They say things like this is where all the information is. These are things you need to know. We really don't want to hear it. You just want your parents and love ones to live forever. It is believed that aging is inevitable. It is said that this is a normal part of life. While most people don't like to think about this. The main thing is have all of your affairs in order. Planning for something like this there are things you need. What happens if your ill or what happens after you die. Especially if your ill and unable to handle some decisions yourself. The things they say you should have in place is a last will and testament. It states what happens with property, affair with the children and name the person who is to carry out all your wishes. Also, you need to have a power of attorney. A person who can take care of all your legal and financial matters. The pain of death is very real----but so is the peace that surrounds us from the Most High. If you find yourself coping with the loss of a loved one, surround yourself with as much support and peace you can. Searching for the answer from the lord through your prayers, by reading the holy book, and for others who support you, where you can find some real hope and comfort. This is a subject I am still coping and working through understanding and coming to total acceptance with. So, what if you could live forever in a place where there was only peace, no sickness, and you could lead a productive life?

Travel

Being able to travel to all the beautiful sites this world has to offer it helps us to understand our place in the world. We can somehow understand more clearly the things we want to create for ourselves. It can make us better sisters, mothers, friends and better wives. Traveling helps keep us humble and helps us learn to tolerate and respect other people and their cultures. We travel sometime to celebrate things like a new job, retirement, class reunion and to be pampered. We take time away to regroup, recharge, and reflect. Trips of adventure test your boundaries and help to develop your confidence to see more of the world and do more things. Traveling to get away and escape from the day to day stresses can be very relaxing. When you travel with you husband or significant other it can keep the spice in your relationship.

It is some fun to plan where you're going and the things you will do when you get there. People have married and renewed vows while on travel. Girlfriend getaways are a popular and wonderful thing to plan and be a part of. They are designed to inspire, empower and lift you up. It brings women together from around the world and from different walks of life to explore the world together and to learn about different cultures. There is so much women empowerment to be harnessed when women get together. To engage, share things they have seen and learned and to listen to one another. On girls getaways you can relax and be your laid-back self. You may need a little break form husband, kids or significant other. You don't have to worry about putting on make-up or shave your legs etc. if you don't want too! You don't have to worry if you gained a few pounds. No one even cares. You can just do your thing. The good thing is none of your girlfriends judge you can do you. That is a beautiful thing! You can do you. It just becomes a fond memory and a funny story to talk about later. Travel as much as you possibly can. Go as far as you can. Life is meant to be lived and not in just one place.

Leisure

Do you feel at this time in your life that you take time out to have leisure time for yourself? For me it is a matter of a balancing act. I think we do need to carve out that leisure time whether you're working or a lady of leisure. Maybe writing down things that you long to do more of ----whether they keep you sane, happy, or relaxed. Making a log of what you do each day to see what you do in a day. Are you spending time on the right things? Think about this: devoting more time on the things you love could possibly help you get more done. If you have you have family members you live with. You could delegate some chores to the children in the home, so you could spend 15 mins. or so doing something more fulfilling with that time. If gives the young child a chance to learn responsibility even when they might protest some of course. Maybe if you can afford it have someone come in and do some house work for you once or twice a week. Also, maybe eliminate some distraction like your PHONE when your home put it up. I know this one is hard for a lot of us. Shut the door. If you have some work to do. Make it clear to everyone concerned you need this time to be left alone. Now maybe after we have freed up some good constructive leisure time. You can decide how you want to spend your energy. Making a daily to do list could be a good start. Take your resting time seriously. Try to be as stress free as you can and make your leisure time just that leisure!

It's Over

I am sure at some point in our lives we had a bad break-up. Whether they broke up with you or you broke up with them. Breaking up is always hard on both people really. Especially when its someone you care about. Its, not just about relationships! You might have had to get rid of a therapist, personal trainer, or housekeeper. It is not easy saying good-bye without completely crushing the persons spirit that you once were in love with and possibly still do love. You could be breaking up with someone who has emotional issues. If your partner could be depressed it seems impossible to do that to them. The problem is you have no control over how the person will take this. You shouldn't stay in this kind of relationship because they make you feel guilt and pity for them. No matter how loving and considerate of these persons feelings you are. There is no easy way to end this one. This will complicate the break-up. After breaking up with the person. You will be tempted to keep in touch with your ex because they are going through depression. It depends on their emotional and mental state as to how well they make it through the break-up. You understand men when women worn you first by telling you we are not happy. This actually gives you a chance to save the relationship. If you pick-up on what we are saying, and you are paying attention. I don't know how you feel about this, but I think your partner deserves a face to face and a discussion with you about why it's over. E-mail, voicemail, text message to me is the cowards way out. Although ending a relationship doesn't make you selfish or bad. It just maybe time to move on. You had your reasons for ending it. Don't let that other person guilt you into staying in relationship for the wrong reasons.

You should give that other person a chance to respond. Ending a relationship of love can have some bitterness, resentment, anger and tears or maybe even no reaction at all. Part of saying that your relationship is over means letting your partner talk about their emotions and feelings. The initial reaction to this might be awkward (even a little painful and scary) but hopefully as time goes on you can talk calmly to one another. Hopefully you can get to a stage that it gets a little easier and you can get to the letting go stage. This would be the ideal thing if you can give your partner time to speak her or his truth. I know at some point we have experienced being "dumped" then you know how crappy that feels. Ending an unhealthy union takes courage and your new chance to start over can change your life for the better. Love yourself and love him and cherish the good times you had together. Don't make it worse by being that person that couldn't let go and wouldn't leave.

Where is my right shoe? (you say one thing and i hear another!)
Billy and Cynthia Powell

THE END!

Where is my right shoe? (you say one thing and i hear another!)
Billy and Cynthia Powell